Meditation For Beginners

How to Meditate For Lifelong Peace, Focus and Happiness

Sara Elliott Price

Published in The USA by:

Success Life Publishing

125 Thomas Burke Dr.

Hillsborough, NC 27278

ISBN-10: 1511850256

Disclaimer

Every effort has been made to accurately represent this book and its potential. Results vary with every individual, and your results may or may not be different from those depicted. No promises, guarantees or warranties, whether stated or implied, have been made that you will produce any specific result from this book. Your efforts are individual and unique, and may vary from those shown. Your success depends on your efforts, background and motivation.

The material in this publication is provided for educational and informational purposes only and is not intended as medical advice. The information contained in this book should not be used to diagnose or treat any illness, metabolic disorder, disease or health problem. Always consult your physician or health care provider before beginning any nutrition or exercise program. Use of the programs, advice, and information contained in this book is at the sole choice and risk of the reader.

Table of Contents

Introduction

You must have heard people talk about the amazing powers of meditation. You might have met people raving about how meditation transformed their life. You might have even read blogs teaching you how to meditate, but when you tried it you found it incredibly frustrating and not peaceful at all.

If that sounds like you, then don't worry because you are not alone--most people feel this way. Meditation is not an easy skill to master. It takes years, if not a lifetime to master this skill. The good news is that you don't have to master it in order to enjoy its benefits.

If you can develop the habit of meditating daily, even for a few minutes, you can achieve wonderful results in your life. Meditation will improve both your physical and mental health, reduce stress, improve your brain power and teach you how to focus your attention on the task at hand, thereby increasing your productivity.

I'm sure not all successful people meditate but you'd be surprised how many of them do some form of meditation. It's an important skill to have for achieving success in life. If you can develop the meditation habit, it will certainly improve your chance of finding success.

An increasing number of scientific studies have been carried out on meditation and almost all of them have shown that meditation can be used to alter brain waves and brain chemistry. But if you are still skeptical, just give meditation a try for a few months. If you meditate daily for just a few months, you'll experience the benefits firsthand and lose your skepticism.

The only problem is that even those who do believe in the powers of meditation find it hard to turn it into a habit. Meditation can be frustrating if you set unrealistic goals for yourself. Most beginners do it the wrong way. They end up thinking that they just can't control their mind enough to meditate and give up. But this doesn't have to be you!

In this book I'll show you how anyone can learn to meditate and how with a little persistence and a systematic approach you, too can develop this seemingly hard habit. After that, it's only a matter of time before you start seeing results. You'll continue to reap the benefits as you get better at meditation. Who knows, someday you may even find enlightenment!

In this book you'll learn:

- What meditation is all about

- The different types of meditation

- How to set yourself up to stick with the meditation habit

- How to meditate as a beginner

- How to move up to higher levels of meditation

- How to build a healthy lifestyle around your habit of meditation

I hope you are ready to learn everything you need to know about meditation. Let's begin by talking a bit about the history of meditation.

Chapter 1: What is Meditation?

The word meditation doesn't have a single concrete meaning. Today this word is used to describe a variety of activities and mental states but the act of meditation has existed since time immemorial in one form or another in every culture in the world.

In the most basic sense, meditation means to concentrate all your attention on something. What that something is, depends on the context in which you are talking about meditation.

History of Meditation

In Hinduism the concept of *Dhyana* has existed since the time of the *Vedas* that were written as early as 1500 BC. *Dhyana* means to be aware of the oneness of the body, mind, soul, and the universe, while remaining completely detached from it all. From Hinduism the concept of *Dhyana* came to Buddhism and Jainism. The Japanese concept of Zen is also closely related to *Dhyana*.

In Yoga, *Pranayama* is a series of breathing exercises that focus on *Prana* or the life force. It is a form of meditation used for healing and relaxation.

In many religions, including Christianity and Judaism, prayer and reading of sacred texts is a form of meditation. In Islam the practice of *Dhikr*, which involves reciting the 99 different names of Allah, has been practiced since the 8th century.

In one form or the other, meditation has existed since us humans walked out of our caves and started building complex societies. In fact, it is said that the ability to focus our attention on a single task for a long time has been a milestone in our evolutionary journey.

Different Types of Meditation

Because of this long and varied history, there are many different forms of meditation that are practiced today. We'll talk about these different types of meditation in more detail in the next chapter but for now it would suffice to list out some of these varying techniques that fall under meditation.

These are:

- Focusing attention on the breath

- Controlling the breath

- Praying and meditating on the name of God

- Controlling your thoughts so as to eliminate thought completely and replace it with a general awareness of the present moment

- Slowing down your thoughts and visualizing a safe place

- Transcendental meditation

- Kundalini meditation

- Practicing mindfulness

- Using prayer beads to recite a mantra a given number of times

- Sound meditation

- Reading sacred texts

- Singing sacred hymns

- Contemplative meditation

- Concentrating on a single task to achieve the feeling of being "in the flow" or "in the zone"

- Focusing attention on your emotions and feeling compassion and gratitude

- New age meditation

As you can see, there are several similar concepts that all fall under the general term meditation. The common factor among all these different types of meditation is that they all have the same purpose; to calm the mind and bring stillness to it that is missing in our normal day to day life.

Have you ever wondered how much work your brain puts in every day? It starts chattering from the moment you wake up. Sometimes you might be half asleep, trying to find the snooze button on the alarm clock, and your brain has already started its non-stop thinking.

Your brain thinks about everything you do during the day. It calculates your every move. It also thinks about past events and creates judgments for the present moment based on your past experience. It then calculates the results of your actions and how they will line up with your dreams for the future. As you go to bed, the brain is still talking at full speed. Sometimes you wish it would just shut up so you can finally get some sleep. And even during sleep, the brain is creating dreams for you to enjoy. When you are not dreaming the subconscious mind is working on the problems you weren't able to solve during the day.

Clearly the brain needs rest. It gets rest only during cycles of deep sleep and even then many parts of the brain are active, running the basic machinery of your body's vital organs.

Meditation allows you to slow down your frantic mind. Things become clear as excess thoughts are lost in the background and only an awareness of the present moment remains. Doing this daily, will help keep your brain healthy, and your mind sane.

There are so many forms of meditation to choose from that it can be overwhelming for the beginner. Which form of meditation you choose, is up to your own personal beliefs but there is a place for most beginners to start from that will help you stick to the meditation habit till you realize the highest benefits.

Benefits of Meditation

Despite all the differences, the benefits of all forms of meditation are almost exactly same. Once you start meditating consistently, no matter which form of meditation, you'll receive the following benefits:

- Your mental health will improve; your thoughts will stop being chaotic and your emotions won't cause an upheaval inside you.

- Anxiety, stress and depression will reduce.

- You'll be more positive.

- You'll be able to concentrate better.

- Your attention span will increase and you'll learn to focus.

- Your mind will slow down and you won't feel like it's running at full speed all the time.

- You'll be able to sleep better.

- Your physical health will improve as your brain sends the right kind of feedback to the body.

- You will be able to stick to a healthier lifestyle and diet, which will help you improve your physical health.

- You will find it easier to stay away from alcohol, tobacco and other bad habits.

- Your productivity and efficiency will increase.

- Your memory power will increase.

- You will be able to make better decisions without being paralyzed by fear.

- As you move to higher levels of meditation you'll get in touch with your real self and find a meaning and purpose to your life which will result in a more fulfilling life.

All these benefits, and more, can be achieved by meditating daily. It will take some time for the results to start showing, and at first it will be hard to stick to, but if you can manage to form this habit, in the end it will all be worth it. Luckily for you, by the time you are done reading this book, you'll know exactly what to expect and how to make this habit stick.

Chapter 2: Choosing the Right Type of Meditation

Out of the different types of meditation, you can choose to begin with the one that resonates the most with you. Maybe you already do some form of meditation but just never thought about it as meditation. The best choice is to start as a beginner and move up to more difficult forms of meditation with time. Before you pick which meditation is best for you, let's talk about the basic types of meditation in a little more detail.

Breath Control

This is a simple form of meditation in which you just focus on your breathing. You concentrate on each breath going in and coming out. You slow down the breathing rate and take longer and deeper breaths.

According to the Hindu concept of *Pranayama,* by controlling your breath you can also control your life force or *Prana.* This leads to immense physical, mental and spiritual health benefits.

But even if you are skeptical about this spiritual concept, scientific studies have shown that breathing deeply and rhythmically can have an immediate effect on both brain and body functions. By breathing slowly you also slow the heart rate and become relaxed. In this state, stress is relieved and

11

the body releases chemicals that help in healing and recovery. Taking deep breaths also oxygenates the body because of the extra air. Highly oxygenated blood circulates through your body and helps in detoxification and healing of all parts of the body.

A lot of the ailments in our body can be healed simply by breathing deeply throughout the day. It isn't that easy to do because we lose awareness and end up breathing short shallow breaths most of the time. Try this the next time you are feeling anxious or nervous, like before an important meeting; take long deep breaths in a rhythmical fashion just before the meeting. You'll find that your anxiety will decrease and you'll perform much better during the meeting.

Breath control meditation utilizes this fact to relieve stress and improve mental abilities. It can also heal the body of physical ailments.

Whichever way you look at it, breath control has a lot of benefits and is relatively easy to do as a beginner.

Thought Control

A higher level of meditation involves slowing and then eliminating all thoughts. This is what most people think all meditation to be but this is just one form of it. It is much harder to do, as you can easily find by trying it once or twice yourself. Our brain is always chatting to us and the thoughts keep flying all the time. When you try to eliminate your thoughts, you start thinking about whether or not your thoughts have reduced and that is a thought in itself, so you are back to square one.

When you try to slow down your thoughts, they start wandering in every which way. To a beginner it can seem impossible that anyone can control, let alone stop all thoughts. Many people try this meditation a few times, fail miserably and feel completely dejected and give up forever. This is a mistake you shouldn't make so avoid this form of meditation in the beginning.

If you can achieve relative control over your thoughts, this is a very powerful form of meditation and can result in tremendous benefits. Scientists have seen a change in brain wave function during such meditation and they are still studying the exact effects of these changes. According to Buddhism, and other spiritual traditions that practice such meditation, you can achieve a blissful state of peace and eventually reach enlightenment or nirvana, by doing this form of meditation.

It also helps in relieving stress and improving brain function. It can help in healing the body as well. All the benefits of breath control are multiplied in thought control along with the extra benefit of eventual enlightenment. Having said that, enlightenment is a hard thing to achieve and most monks spend their lifetime meditating without reaching it.

It's best to avoid this form of meditation in the beginning. Once you get a little better with breath control, you can slowly move up to thought control.

Devotional Meditation

If you are a religious person, then chances are that you already pray. Wise men have always said that there is a lot of power in prayer and there's a good reason for that. Prayer, when done right, is just another form of meditation. There are many forms to prayer itself and all of them are powerful. Just taking a few minutes to say thanks can heal the heart if you feel genuine gratitude.

Wishing someone well in your prayers can help you feel compassion, which has its own benefits. The trick is to feel the prayer from within and not just to recite the words. Using prayer beads to repeat a mantra or the name of God for a few minutes is very similar to meditation. It will help you focus your mind and since you'll be concentrating on God you won't have any other thoughts. Reading sacred texts with full concentration is also a form of devotional meditation.

The benefits of this are similar to other forms of meditation and depend on how sincerely you pray. This is a good way to initiate yourself into meditation if you have faith in one or another religion. Since religion is involved, it will also be easier for you to stick to the habit because everyone can make time for God. But if you are an agnostic or a complete atheist then this obviously won't work for you. But don't worry because when it comes to meditation, there's something for everyone.

Mindfulness

Another form of meditation is known as mindfulness. This simply means to bring your attention to the present moment. Instead of thinking about the past or the future, you bring your mind to the present moment. You don't think about what your spouse said or what your boss wants you to do, instead you focus on the task at hand. By doing this you control your thoughts from rushing in random directions. You still have thoughts but they are related only to the present moment.

You are allowed to think about how you feel right now, how your body feels, what each of your sense organs observes etc. You can think about the sights, the smells and the sounds. You can think about whatever it is that you are doing but you can't think about the past or the future.

This is a simple and incredibly powerful way of meditating and controlling your thoughts. It is also harder to do than it sounds. The good thing about mindfulness is that you can practice it while doing anything. You can start by practicing it while taking a walk or just sitting quietly in a peaceful spot. But later on you can begin to stay mindful throughout the day no matter what you are doing.

It is easy to become lost in your work when you love what you are doing. Sportsmen and musicians talk about being in the zone, where they forget about everything else and only focus on the present moment. They'll tell you that this experience doesn't just help them perform better but also fills them up with a kind of peace that is hard to achieve in daily life. It's blissful and nothing short of a spiritual experience. But you can practice mindfulness and have the same experience even while doing something boring or dull. You can experience it even while washing dishes, if you only pay complete attention to the present moment and don't think about anything else.

This type of meditation will help you release stress and become positive and happy. It will also increase your productivity and the ability to focus and concentrate. You can try it simultaneously while forming a more formal meditation habit. To do this you just have to remind yourself repeatedly through the day to pay attention to the present moment and not to think about the past or the future.

Miscellaneous

Some other forms of meditation that you can try are:

- **Transcendental Meditation:** This is one of the most famous forms of meditation in the world today and was started in the 60s by Maharishi Mahesh Yogi. The technique involves meditating with your eyes closed and using the sound of a mantra to concentrate. It is practiced for 15 to 20 minutes twice everyday. It helps in reducing stress and increasing relaxation. You can learn transcendental meditation from certified teachers of the TM organization.

- **Kundalini Meditation:** This form of meditation is based on the concept of Kundalini; a spiritual energy that lies at the base of the spine. Kundalini meditation focuses on awakening this energy which is said to heal the body, mind and the soul and can help you realize your potential as a spiritual being.

- **Sound Meditation:** This form of meditation uses audio to focus attention. The audio can be a mantra or a song or even just peaceful instrumental music. You can also choose to do assisted meditation in which you listen to a recording of a master taking you step by step through the meditation. This is mostly used for relaxation and stress release.

- **Compassionate Meditation:** A related form of the Kundalini meditation is the compassionate meditation, also sometimes known as the heart chakra meditation. In this form of meditation you focus on the feelings of compassion and gratitude. These emotions can be targeted towards an individual, yourself, God, humanity, life or the universe in general. You imagine your heart filling with this compassionate energy and then you release it into the world. This form of meditation is wonderful for people going through an emotionally challenging time.

Best for Beginners

As you can see there are a lot of different ideologies to choose from. As a beginner its best to begin with breath control as a daily practice. You can also try to be mindful throughout the day as it will only help you in the long run. But the daily practice that you turn into a habit should be the breath control form of meditation.

It is easy to do and when you focus your attention on your breath, your thoughts automatically slow down. It is a good way to build concentration and slowly move into thought control meditation. In the beginning the importance should be

18

towards building a habit and not so much on how well you can meditate or if you can do the hardest meditation or not. As you get deeper into meditation, and once you have a strong habit and have seen the results for yourself, you can then explore all other forms of meditation according to what appeals the most to you.

Chapter 3: Preparing for the Meditation Habit

Good preparation guarantees success in any endeavor. Before you begin to incorporate the habit of meditation into your life, you should prepare yourself for the change. This will improve your chances of sticking with the habit till you start seeing positive results.

Decide to Stick with It

First of all, you need to make the decision to give meditation a serious try. Many people hear about meditation and think halfheartedly about trying it out. They sit for a few minutes to try and silence their mind but it doesn't work. They try it for a few days and then either get busy or just give up, thinking that it's all just hokum. If you approach meditation with such an attitude, you are guaranteed to fail.

If you truly want to receive the benefits of meditation then you need to give it enough time to work. You need to make a strong decision that you are going to try out mediation for the next 3-6 months. Be determined from the start to not quit even if you don't see any results at all.

Visualize Results

It can help to visualize the benefits you'll receive from meditation. As mentioned earlier in this book, you'll be less stressed and have a calm and collected mind, once you form the meditation habit. Imagine yourself at work; you can focus completely on the task at hand and don't get distracted. Your work impresses your boss. Or imagine your body cleansing itself of all toxins and negativity with each breath during mediation. When you'll keep these benefits in mind, you'll be able to stick to meditation for a longer time.

Reduce Negativity

It will also help if you decrease negative stimuli in your life even before you begin meditating. Alcohol and tobacco don't go well with meditation. I hope I don't have to mention that neither do drugs. If you can reduce these stimulants from your life before you begin meditating, it will improve your chances of seeing fast results.

TV and internet are both a source of another form of stimulant that hinders meditation. That stimulant is excessive information. We live in the age of information overload, which can lead to a chaotic mind. Try to reduce the amount of information you take in before you start meditating. In the beginning you want to do everything you can to make your mind calm for meditation. Once you get good at meditating, it will help you keep your mind calm even in the most chaotic situations.

Choose a Time

You need to choose a fixed time for meditation that you can easily stick to everyday. The best time is early morning but if you aren't a morning person, you can choose any other time of the day. The earlier it is in the day, the easier it will be to calm your mind. After a long hard day's work, it is much harder to meditate but it doesn't mean that you can't meditate at night. If that's the best time for you, then go ahead and choose it. Whatever suits your routine so that you are confident of not missing it too often is good.

When you'll start meditating, try to stick to this fixed time as often as you can. If you miss the set time for some reason, it's okay to meditate at a different time as well. But don't make it a habit to meditate at a different time everyday. Instead set a fixed time early in the day and a back up time in the evening so that in case you miss the first appointment, you still have a chance to put in the day's meditation session.

Choose a Place

Along with a set time, if you can set a fixed place to meditate, it would help in sticking to the habit. Create a small space in one corner of your bedroom, or maybe out in the yard, or even in a park; whatever works for you. Choose a place where you can sit in peace without being disturbed. There's no need to build a soundproof room for meditation. Any sound is okay as long as it is not too distracting. So if you can hear traffic in the distance, that's okay but you might not want to meditate right on the sidewalk of a busy intersection.

Choose the Duration

Before starting meditation, you also need to decide how long you are going to meditate for. I recommend anywhere between 3 to 5 minutes for beginners. It seems like a very short amount of time, but you'll be surprised how hard it is to meditate even for such a short time without your mind running off several times. Even 3 minutes of good meditation can show tremendous results. Slowly, as you increase your level, you can start meditating for longer periods.

By choosing a set amount of time, you remove the uncertainty of how long you are supposed to meditate. Use a timer to track your time and don't keep looking at the watch to see if your 3 minutes have passed.

Tell Others

Once you decide to begin meditation, let your family members know about your intentions. Make them understand that it is important to you and if possible, ask them to join you. Having a family member be part of this journey will make it special and fun for both of you. But even if they don't want to be a part of this journey, at least help them understand that you don't want to be disturbed during your meditation time. Let them know your time and place of meditation so they can stay clear.

It can help if you also declare your intentions to your friends and even to the rest of the world. This can help you stay accountable for your decision and motivate you to stick with it. The same internet that overloads us with information can come in handy here as you can share your journey through social media. Write a blog about your experience as it can be very encouraging to share your journey with like minded individuals.

With these tips in mind you can prepare yourself in a way that will make it easy to stick to meditation long enough for it to show positive results. In the next chapter we'll finally talk about how to meditate.

Chapter 4: The Meditation Habit

You are now ready to begin your meditation practice on a regular basis. At the set time, go to your chosen place and get ready to meditate. It helps to stretch a little before meditation, as loosening the body will help you to sit comfortably. It is important to be comfortable because only then can you calm your mind. Wear comfortable clothes and turn off all distractions such as the phone or any other device. Only the timer should be used to keep track of time. Keep it out of reach so that you don't compulsively check it to see how much time is left. Take off your shoes and keep them aside. Try to calm the mind and avoid thinking about anything else except the present moment.

Posture

The position you sit in is important but it is not necessary to sit cross-legged if you can't do it easily. Sitting on a chair can also work but you have to remember that you must keep your spine fairly straight. Assume a confident and rigid yet relaxed position. If you are sitting on a chair, keep your feet side by side on the floor. Do not cross your feet or raise the heels. You can keep your hands on your lap in a relaxed position.

If you choose to sit cross-legged, make sure you are comfortable. The spine should again be straight. You should be looking straight ahead so that your neck is in line with the spine. Keep your hands rested on your knees, facing downwards. If you want, you can turn them upwards with the forefinger touching the thumb to form the traditional lotus position. These little postures are supposed to increase the benefits of meditation but it is not necessary to do them. The most important thing is to be comfortable.

The Practice

To begin meditation, close your eyes and slowly turn your attention inwards. In the beginning, just observe yourself. Start by observing your body; go over each body part starting from the toes and finishing at the head and observe how each part feels. If any muscles feel tense, try to relax them. If you need to, change the position in which you are sitting.

Observe how your chest feels. If it feels constricted, like a weight is placed on it, take a deep breath and expand your chest as much as possible. Feel the weight lift off of your chest. If your thoughts are rushing, don't get frustrated. Instead try to be calm and slowly bring your focus back to the task at hand.

The task at hand is to concentrate on the breath. Just observe the breath in the beginning. Feel it enter your lungs and see how deep you normally breathe. If you observe a newborn baby breathing, you'll see that it breathes from its stomach, but as we grow up, we start breathing from our chests. Our breathing is very restricted and we only take shallow breaths in which our chest expands only slightly.

During meditation, you need to ensure that you are breathing deep and long. Breathe in as much as you can and then hold for as long as you can. While breathing out make sure that you do it slowly and in a controlled way. Don't rush it. Breathe out till your stomach contracts inwards and then hold for a while.

Focus on this cycle of breathing in, holding, breathing out, and holding. This will automatically reduce your breathing rate while increasing the amount of oxygen that is going in your body. As your breathing slows down, your heartbeat will also slow and your mind will stop rushing. You can experience this peaceful state even on the first day.

In the beginning, it will be hard to hold on to this state. You'll find that soon your mind gets distracted and your breathing returns to normal shallow bursts. To stay focused, count each breathing cycle every time you inhale. Count up to 5 and then restart from 1. This will help you stay focused for longer but still you can be sure that you will get distracted.

Don't try to force this state of concentration. The more you try to hold on to it, the harder it will be. Most importantly, don't beat yourself up for not being able to stay focused. It is completely normal to have a rushing mind. This is how everybody feels. But with practice you can train your mind to slow down and stay focused on one task at a time. You just need to be patient and treat yourself as a child learning a new skill. You don't shout at kids for drawing outside the lines. In the same way you must be gentle, kind and encouraging to yourself when you are learning to control your mind.

Finishing Meditation

Once the set time is over, slowly open your eyes. Don't be in a rush to get up and enter normal life again. Take some time to just be there. Observe your surroundings and let your thoughts run free. Before getting up, you should try to say thanks and feel compassion and gratitude for being alive. This is also a good time to say any positive affirmations about your goals and life.

This is the simple practice that you need to do daily. Still many people find it hard to turn it into a habit. In the next chapter we'll talk about how to stick to this habit so that it is ingrained into your daily routine. We'll also talk about how to take things to the next level.

Chapter 5: Moving Forward

As you saw in the last chapter, the meditation practice itself is really simple. Yet many people find it difficult to turn it into a habit. That's because they don't stick with it long enough. Here are a few tips that will help you stick with the habit of meditation:

- **Never miss 3 days in a row.** That should be your maximum allowance. Since the practice is so simple and only takes a few minutes, there is no real excuse to miss even a single day. Having said that, sometimes there are genuine reasons to miss the practice. But make sure that if you miss it two days in a row, you must do it on the third day.

- **Start small and be patient.** In the beginning you might feel that you breezed through the 5 minute session. But don't be in a hurry to increase the amount of time. Be patient and stick with short and simple sessions at least for the first 3 months. If you increase the amount of time too soon, it can lead to frustration and you'll be more likely to quit.

- **Don't quit just because you think it's not working.** After a few months of doing meditation regularly, you might feel that there hasn't been any perceptible change in your life. You might feel that you are peaceful during the meditation sessions but it hasn't translated into anything meaningful in your life. Well guess what, it takes time to make changes to your life. You should start with the commitment to do meditation for 3-6 months even if you don't observe any real benefits. If you feel peaceful for just a few minutes, then that alone is reason enough to meditate.

- **Don't get frustrated.** If you don't feel peaceful during meditation and instead feel frustration for your failure to focus, you need to calm down. Meditation is not a competition. It is not a sport where you have to achieve certain results to be deemed a "winner". You can't win at meditation. The only goal of meditation is to do the act of meditation. Don't get frustrated at your failures. Instead just do your best and be patient. Slowly you will improve control over your brain. It is a highly trainable muscle. We unknowingly train it to keep running at full speed all the time but you can just as easily retrain it to be thoughtless.

- **Stick to the same routine.** The brain likes familiar routines so once you have formed a routine where you mediate for a certain amount of time at a fixed time and at the same place, then stick to it. This will help you meditate better because as soon as it is time to meditate the brain will prepare itself to become calm and relaxed. Your brain will begin to enjoy these moments of stillness and it will be easy to stick to the habit.

Once you feel confident that you have more or less ingrained the habit of meditation, it's time to move forward on to the higher levels of meditation. Here's how to do this:

- **Make sure that you are able to spend most of your meditation time focused on your breath.** It's not about increasing the amount of time you spend meditating but more about how long you are focused and how much of the time you are distracted. When you feel confident that you can stay focused for extended periods of time, you are ready to move on.

- **Begin by just watching your thoughts.** You should still start your meditation with breath control and once you have slowed down your breathing a bit, let it go on autopilot and focus on your thoughts. At this time just observe the thoughts without trying to slow them down.

- **Observe the thoughts without judgment.** The idea is to try and detach yourself from your thoughts. When you think about some person, the emotional reactions related to that person should not arise in your mind.

31

- In order to achieve detachment, **try and think of your mind as a movie theatre** and your thoughts are the movie that is being played. Just watch like a spectator, without trying to control the direction in which the movie goes.

- **You don't need to suppress your emotions either.** Let them arise but try to stay detached. A good way to do this is to observe the thoughts, and their reactions, from a distance, instead of flowing along with them.

- This is easier said than done and when you try it for the first time, you might feel that it's impossible to detach yourself from your thoughts and emotions. But **keep at it and don't try to rush it**. With consistent practice you will be able to do this.

- Once you learn to detach yourself from the thoughts, it's time to try and slow them down. Just **by observing your thoughts from a distance you'll slow them down** a bit. This is because one part of you will be thinking the thoughts and the other part will be thinking about those thoughts. In normal everyday life these parts of the brain, all try to think random thoughts and you feel like you are trying to catch several butterflies at the same time.

- Another good way to slow down thoughts is to **stop thinking in words and start thinking in pictures**. Most people think in words. There is always a brain chatter going on inside. If you observe carefully, you'll find that there are two, or sometimes more, voice tracks inside your head. The first one is the loud track that constantly talks about whatever main thought has arisen in your mind. The second track is more subtle and sometimes talks about other thoughts and sometimes gives commentary on the first track. If you try to visualize every thought instead of verbalizing it, then you can considerably slow down your thoughts because it is harder to visualize thoughts at high speed.

- An important thing to note is that the language center is in the left hemisphere and when we think in words we are mostly using our left hemisphere which we use all the time during our normal day. **By switching to pictures we use the right hemisphere and give the left hemisphere a break.** You'll also find that while the left hemisphere is good at dividing things into neat little segments, the right hemisphere looks at the bigger picture. A lot of meditation is about balancing the use of both hemispheres to live a more wholesome life.

- When your thoughts have slowed down, you need to **just be in that state**. You can't try to be thoughtless because as soon as you think about being thoughtless, a thought has arisen in your mind. It's a paradox according to which you can only become aware of a thoughtless state after it is over. If you keep meditating this way for a long time, soon you'll have short moments of complete silence in your mind. The moment you realize that your mind is silent; the silence will break because of the thought about being silent. With practice you can begin to increase these little silent moments.

- **Remember that it takes years for Buddhist monks to reach this level.** And they meditate all the time. For you it might take a lifetime but it can be achieved. The benefits of achieving this level of meditation are immeasurable. Imagine having the power to experience bliss everyday. This level is like the moment of orgasm, where you are completely thoughtless and still completely aware of the present moment. You are completely in the moment and it is pure bliss. Imagine if you could feel this way all the time! With meditation it is possible.

I've mentioned the process here in short, but in reality it will take many years to move up each step. You have to understand that meditation is a lifestyle choice and once you commit to it, you do so for life. In the next chapter, I'll give you some final tips to make the most of the mediation habit.

Chapter 6: Additional Tips

Meditation is a way to still the mind. In today's age we all can use some stillness. A lot of today's problems; depression, anxiety, attention deficit disorder, stress etc. are all due to the superfast pace of our lives. When the mind doesn't get to be still for too long, it can't stay healthy. Once negativity settles in, it creates a negative feedback loop in which the negativity feeds on itself and keeps growing. But with the help of meditation you can create a positive feedback loop and get out of this hole.

If you are still skeptical about meditation, at least give it a try for 3 months and then decide for yourself. As I've shown in the book, it is not that hard to build the meditation habit. It doesn't take a lot of time and doesn't require you to spend any money to buy special equipment. If you meditate consistently for a good period of time, you will definitely see great results.

Here are some additional tips that will help you in making the most of meditation:

- **Meditation goes well with a healthy lifestyle.** Chances are that if you are reading this book then you too want to achieve self-improvement in all areas of your life. The good news is that meditation provides a positive feedback cycle that will help you achieve self-improvement in other areas as well. When you meditate daily, your lifestyle will become healthy and when your lifestyle becomes healthy you will be able to meditate with that much more focus.

- **Start exercising** to go along with meditation. This will ensure complete physical and mental fitness.

- **Control what you eat.** Our thoughts are influenced by what we eat. If you eat healthy it will be easier to have positive thoughts. If you eat a lot of junk food, your mind will be chaotic and full of negativity. If possible, become a vegetarian. Meat of all sorts, especially which is obtained from factory farms, has a lot of negative energy from all the violence behind it. A vegetarian diet is more spiritual and will help you meditate better.

- **Try aromatherapy** during meditation. Light a scented candle and include your sense of smell in meditation. After a while, the scent will work like a cue for your brain to quiet down and prepare for meditation.

- **Meditate early in the morning,** if you can, because that is the quietest time of the day and your mind is relatively free of thoughts. If you clear your head the first thing in the morning, you can have a great time throughout the rest of the day.

- **Meditate during sunrise** because sunrise has a lot of positive energy and it will fill you with positivity as well.

- Try to **apply mindfulness throughout the day**. It's as simple as reminding yourself to stay focused on one task at a time. Do not multitask. Leave that to the computers.

- **Learn to play a musical instrument**, if you don't already, as it is another way to teach your brain to focus and achieve meditation.

- **Sleep 8 hours daily.** While meditation we try to achieve stillness for the brain but it is during deep sleep that the brain gets its real rest. Adequate sleep ensures a healthy mind and body. If you don't sleep properly, your brain will start loosing its attention power and it will be near impossible to meditate.

- As you begin to include meditation in your daily life, **start exploring spirituality** and other related ideas such as yoga. The more spiritual your life becomes, the easier it will be to meditate.

- **Do not try to achieve thoughtlessness directly.** You have to approach it sideways. It's like a mirage that you can only see from the side of your eyes. As soon as you look directly at it, the mirage disappears. When you stop trying to achieve thoughtlessness and only focus on slowing down your thoughts, only then can you achieve it.

These tips will help you develop an overall healthy and spiritual lifestyle that will ensure that you stay stress free and live life to the fullest. That's all you need to know about the meditation habit and how to develop it in your own life.

Conclusion

I hope this book has convinced you to give the meditation habit a wholehearted try. Whether you are religious, simply spiritual, agnostic, or even an atheist, there is something for everyone in meditation.

Think of it what you will; a way to connect with God, a method of awakening your spirit, or just a method of relaxation and stress relief. Whatever your point of view, you can still reap the benefits of meditation by forming the meditation habit.

Meditation is a spiritual pursuit but you don't have to be a spiritualist to reap its benefits. The positive effects on mental and physical health are enough reason for even the strongest rationalist to try meditation.

As I've shown, it's very easy to form this habit as long as you are patient and set the right expectations from the start. Persevere long enough and you'll start noticing reduced stress, better mental health, positivity, increase in concentration power and improved productivity.

I wish you all the best in your personal development journey and I hope that meditation will become an important and reliable tool in your self-improvement toolkit.

57027393R00027

Made in the USA
Lexington, KY
05 November 2016